A Year to Re

1984

For Those Whose Hearts Belong to 1984

Celebrating your year

1984

A memorable year for

Contents

Introduction

A Year to Remember - 1984
For Those Whose Hearts Belong to 1984

To our cherished readers who hold a special connection to the year 1984, whether it's because you were born in this remarkable year, celebrated a milestone, or hold dear memories from that time, this book is a tribute to you and your unique connection to an unforgettable era.

In the pages that follow, we invite you to embark on a captivating journey back to 1984, a year of profound historical significance. For those with a personal connection to this year, it holds a treasure trove of memories, stories, and experiences that shaped the world and touched your lives.

Throughout this book, we've woven together the tapestry of 1984, providing historical insights, personal stories, and interactive activities that allow you to relive and celebrate the significance of this special year.

As you turn the pages and immerse yourself in the events and culture of 1984, we hope you'll find moments of nostalgia, inspiration, and the opportunity to rekindle cherished memories of this extraordinary year.

This book is dedicated to you, our readers, who share a unique bond with 1984. May it bring you joy, enlightenment, and a deeper connection to the rich tapestry of history that weaves through your lives.

With warm regards,
Edward Art Lab

Chapter 1:
Politics and Leading Events around the World

1.1 The Global Stage in 1984: Where Were You?

The year 1984 was marked by a series of pivotal events that unfolded on the global stage, leaving an indelible mark on history. From political assassinations to groundbreaking agreements, here's a concise look at some of the significant occurrences that shaped the world in 1984:

Indian Prime Minister Indira Gandhi Assassinated:

In 1984, the assassination of Indian Prime Minister Indira Gandhi shocked the world. She was assassinated by two of her own bodyguards, leading to a period of political uncertainty and unrest in India.

Hong Kong Handover Agreement:

In December 1984, the United Kingdom and China reached an agreement on the future of Hong Kong. It was decided that Hong Kong would be handed back to China in 1997, marking the end of British colonial rule. The agreement established a "one country, two systems" framework for Hong Kong's governance.

Miner's Strike in England:

During 1984, a significant and year-long miner's strike took place in England. It was marked by labor disputes and protests within the mining industry, leading to significant social and economic consequences.

Royal Diplomacy: Queen Elizabeth II's Visit to Jordan, 1984

On the 26th of March 1984, a significant and diplomatic event unfolded as Queen Elizabeth II of the United Kingdom and her consort, Prince Philip, arrived at Amman Military Airport in Amman, Jordan. This visit marked the beginning of a five-day sojourn to the Kingdom of Jordan.

Upon their arrival, Queen Elizabeth II was resplendent in a pink coat and a white hat adorned with a floral detail, while King Hussein of Jordan, attired in a military uniform, warmly welcomed her. This meeting between two heads of state symbolized the strong ties and diplomatic relations between their respective nations.

The visit of Queen Elizabeth II and Prince Philip to Jordan was not only a symbol of goodwill but also a testament to the importance of international diplomacy and collaboration. It underscored the enduring bonds between the United Kingdom and Jordan, fostering cultural exchange, mutual respect, and shared values.

A Royal Mother's Pride: Queen Elizabeth II Presents Polo Award to Prince Charles, Prince of Wales

On the 30th of July 1984, a touching and memorable moment unfolded on the polo fields of Smiths Lawn in Windsor, Berkshire, England. It was a day when familial bonds and sporting achievement intersected in a heartwarming scene. Charles, Prince of Wales, the eldest son of Queen Elizabeth II, was presented with an award by his mother, the reigning monarch.

The event in question was a polo match, a sport beloved by Prince Charles, who was an accomplished polo player. After a hard-fought and successful match, Queen Elizabeth II took the opportunity to honor her son's sporting prowess by presenting him with an award.

This gesture exemplified not only the Queen's maternal pride but also her recognition of her son's dedication and skill in the world of polo. It was a public display of their close relationship, and it highlighted the Queen's support for her family's interests and endeavors.

First Untethered Spacewalk:

In the realm of space exploration, 1984 witnessed the first untethered spacewalk, a remarkable achievement that allowed an astronaut to maneuver freely in space without being connected to the spacecraft.

1.2 Leaders and Statesmen: Movers and Shakers of '84

The year 1984 saw the world stage graced by leaders and statesmen who played pivotal roles in shaping the course of history. From their political prowess to their diplomatic finesse, these figures left an indelible mark on their respective nations and the international arena:

Indira Gandhi (India):

Indira Gandhi, the charismatic and formidable Prime Minister of India, continued to be a dominant force in Indian politics in 1984. Her leadership was marked by both triumph and tragedy. While she achieved success in foreign policy and economic reforms, her tragic assassination in October sent shockwaves through the nation.

Margaret Thatcher (United Kingdom):

Margaret Thatcher, often referred to as the "Iron Lady," remained at the helm of the United Kingdom's government in 1984. Her conservative policies, including privatization and a strong stance on the Falklands War, defined her tenure as Prime Minister.

Zhao Ziyang (China):

Zhao Ziyang, the Premier of the People's Republic of China, was instrumental in negotiating the historic Sino-British Joint Declaration in 1984. This agreement paved the way for the peaceful transfer of sovereignty over Hong Kong from the UK to China in 1997, introducing the concept of "one country, two systems."

Arthur Scargill (United Kingdom):

Arthur Scargill, the leader of the National Union of Mineworkers (NUM), played a central role in the year-long miner's strike in England. His efforts to protect miners' rights and job security led to one of the most significant labor disputes in British history.

Haile Selassie (Ethiopia):

Emperor Haile Selassie of Ethiopia faced the daunting challenge of addressing a severe famine and political conflicts in 1984. His leadership during this crisis drew international attention and humanitarian efforts to alleviate the suffering in Ethiopia.

Warren E. Burger (United States):

Warren E. Burger served as the Chief Justice of the United States Supreme Court in 1984. His tenure was marked by several landmark decisions, including those related to civil rights, privacy, and constitutional law.

Richard Branson (United Kingdom):

Richard Branson, the entrepreneurial spirit behind Virgin Group, achieved a significant feat in 1984 by completing the first solo transatlantic flight in a helium balloon. His daring adventure showcased the boundless possibilities of air travel.

Activity: Historical Crossword st Your Knowledge of '84

Are you ready to challenge your knowledge of the significant events and key figures of 1984? Here's a crossword puzzle that will test your understanding of the historic year.

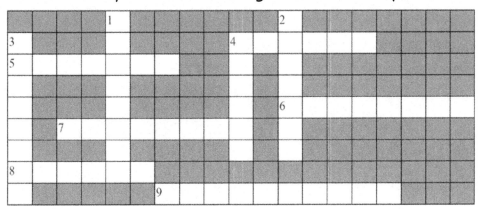

ACROSS

4. Chief Justice of the United States Supreme Court in 1984
5. Year-long miner's strike in this country in 1984
6. Leader of the National Union of Mineworkers during the miner's strike in 1984
7. Country where a widespread famine occurred in 1984
8. Indian Prime Minister assassinated in 1984
9. Chinese Premier who negotiated the Hong Kong agreement in 1984

DOWN

1. UK's Prime Minister known as the "Iron Lady" in 1984
2. Entrepreneur who completed the first solo transatlantic flight in a helium balloon in 1984
3. Emperor of Ethiopia who faced a severe famine in 1984
4. Location of the Bhopal gas tragedy in 1984

Chapter 2:
The Iconic Movies, TV Shows, and Awards

In the realm of entertainment, the year 1984 was marked by an array of iconic films, captivating TV shows, and prestigious awards that left a lasting impact on pop culture. Let's delve into the cinematic and small-screen highlights of '84:

2.1 Memorable Films of '84

Ghostbusters

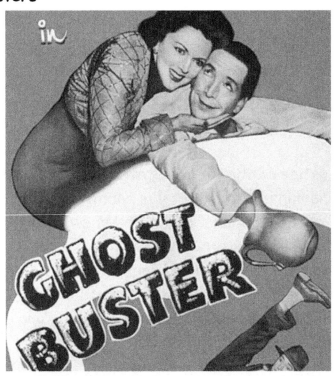

Directed by Ivan Reitman, "Ghostbusters" combined supernatural elements with comedy, featuring the hilarious trio of Bill Murray, Dan Aykroyd, and Harold Ramis. Their witty banter and ghost-busting antics charmed audiences, making this film an instant classic.

Indiana Jones and the Temple of Doom

Harrison Ford reprised his role as the adventurous archaeologist Indiana Jones in this Steven Spielberg-directed sequel. The film's daring action sequences, exotic locales, and memorable characters kept viewers on the edge of their seats.

Gremlins

Directed by Joe Dante, "Gremlins" took a darkly comedic twist on a classic tale. The mischievous Gremlins, spawned from adorable Mogwai, wreaked havoc in a small town during the holiday season, blending humor with horror.

Beverly Hills Cop:

Eddie Murphy's star power shone brightly in this action-comedy, where he portrayed Axel Foley, a Detroit cop navigating the glitzy streets of Beverly Hills. Murphy's charismatic performance and humorous escapades made this film a box office hit.

The Karate Kid

Directed by John G. Avildsen, this coming-of-age story followed the journey of Daniel LaRusso, played by Ralph Macchio, as he learned martial arts and life lessons from Mr. Miyagi, portrayed by Pat Morita. The film's underdog tale resonated with audiences and spawned a beloved franchise.

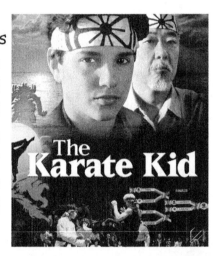

Star Trek III: The Search for Spock

The Enterprise crew, led by Captain Kirk (William Shatner), embarked on a mission to rescue Spock (Leonard Nimoy) in this sci-fi adventure directed by Nimoy himself. The film continued the legacy of the "Star Trek" franchise.

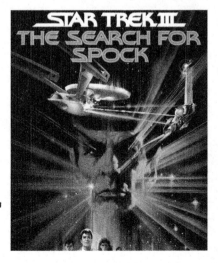

Police Academy

This comedy, directed by Hugh Wilson, introduced viewers to a diverse group of police recruits, each with their quirks and eccentricities. The film's zany humor and memorable characters paved the way for a successful franchise.

The Terminator

James Cameron's sci-fi thriller introduced audiences to a relentless cyborg assassin, the Terminator, portrayed by Arnold Schwarzenegger. The film's blend of action, suspense, and futuristic themes made it a cult classic.

2.2 TV Shows That Captivated the Nation

Television in 1984 was a tapestry of drama, intrigue, and entertainment, with TV shows that not only captivated the nation but also became cultural touchstones:

Magnum, P.I

Tom Selleck's portrayal of the charming private investigator Thomas Magnum in the scenic backdrop of Hawaii made this series a fan favorite. Viewers tuned in for Magnum's adventures and witty one-liners.

Dynasty

A glamorous and dramatic saga of the wealthy Carrington family, "Dynasty" delved into power struggles, family dynamics, and opulent lifestyles. The show's larger-than-life characters became household names.

Entertainment Tonight

This iconic entertainment news program, hosted by Mary Hart and John Tesh, provided an exclusive behind-the-scenes look at the world of celebrities, Hollywood premieres, and entertainment events.

Falcon Crest

Set in the wine industry, "Falcon Crest" was a soap opera filled with family rivalries, romantic entanglements, and dramatic plot twists. The show kept viewers enthralled with its intricate storytelling.

Hill Street Blues

A groundbreaking police procedural series, "Hill Street Blues" focused on the lives of police officers, tackling complex issues and introducing character-driven storytelling that set a new standard for TV dramas.

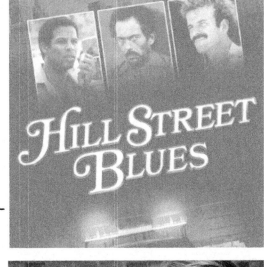

Cagney and Lacey

This police procedural drama featured two female detectives, Sharon Gless and Tyne Daly, as they navigated the challenges of their male-dominated profession while solving crimes. The show addressed social issues and earned critical acclaim.

Jeopardy!

Hosted by Alex Trebek, "Jeopardy!" continued to challenge contestants' knowledge and quick thinking with its unique quiz show format.

Cheers

The beloved sitcom set in the Cheers bar, where "everybody knows your name," became a cultural phenomenon. The witty banter and endearing characters, including Sam Malone (Ted Danson) and Diane Chambers (Shelley Long), resonated with viewers.

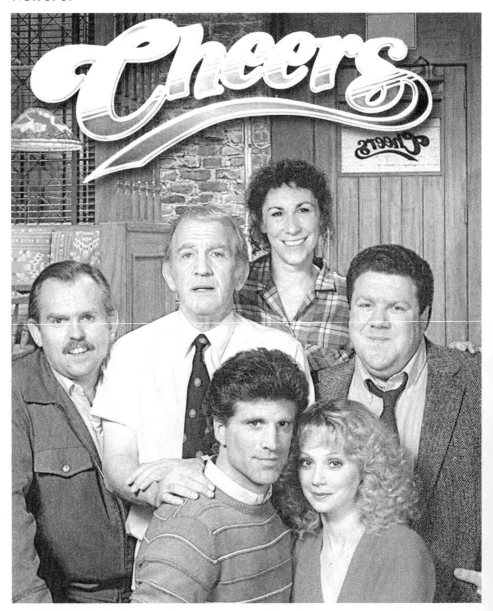

2.3 Prestigious Film Awards and Honors

The world of cinema celebrated excellence in filmmaking in 1984, with prestigious awards and honors recognizing outstanding contributions:

The 56th Academy Awards:

Category	Winner
Best Picture	Terms of Endearment
Best Director	James L. Brooks (Terms of Endearment)
Best Actor in a Leading Role	RSobert Duvall (Tender Mercies)
Best Actress in a Leading Role	Shirley MacLaine (Terms of Endearment)
Best Actor in a Supporting Role	Jack Nicholson (Terms of Endearment)
Best Actress in a Supporting Role	Linda Hunt (The Year of Living Dangerously)
Best Screenplay Written Directly for the Screen	Horton Foote(Tender Mercies)
Best Screenplay Based on Material from Another Medium	James L. Brooks (Terms of Endearment)

The Golden Globe Awards recognized achievements in film and television, with "Terms of Endearment" and its stars earning accolades.

The Cannes Film Festival featured notable entries, with Wim Wenders' "Paris, Texas" winning the Palme d'Or.

The BAFTA Awards celebrated British and international films, with "Educating Rita" and "Terms of Endearment" among the winners.

The Emmy Awards recognized excellence in television, with "Hill Street Blues" dominating the drama categories.

Activity:
Movie and TV Show Trivia Quiz
How Well Do You Know '84 Entertainment?

Let's test your knowledge of the iconic movies and TV shows from 1984! Take this trivia quiz and see how well you remember the entertainment highlights of that year.

1.Who directed the supernatural comedy"Ghostbusters"?

A) Steven Spielberg

B) Ivan Reitman

C) Joe Dante

D) James Cameron

2. In "Indiana Jones and the Temple of Doom," who played the role of Indiana Jones?

A) Harrison Ford

B) Arnold Schwarzenegger

C) Tom Cruise

D) Mel Gibson

3. "Gremlins" took a comedic twist on a classic tale. What were the mischievous creatures called?

A) Hobbits

B) Gremlins

C) Mogwai

D) Goblins

4. In "Beverly Hills Cop," which actor portrayed the charming Detroit cop, Axel Foley?

A) Eddie Murphy   C) Dan Aykroyd

B) Bill Murray   D) Harold Ramis

5. What life lessons did Daniel LaRusso learn in "The Karate Kid"?

A) Karate

B) Martial arts and car repair

C) Ballet

D) Swimming

6. Which TV series featured Tom Selleck as the charming private investigator Thomas Magnum?

A) Falcon Crest

B) Hill Street Blues

C) Magnum, P.I.

D) Cheers

7. "Dynasty" revolved around the lives of which wealthy family?

A) The Carringtons

B) The Ewings

C) The Tates

D) The Colbys

8. What iconic entertainment news program provided behind-the-scenes looks at Hollywood and celebrities?

A) Entertainment Weekly

B) Access Hollywood

C) Entertainment Tonight

D) TMZ

9. In "Hill Street Blues," what was the show's focus?

A) Legal drama

B) Medical drama

C) Police procedural

D) Sci-fi adventure

10. Who hosted the quiz show "Jeopardy!" in 1984?
A) Pat Sajak
B) Alex Trebek
C) Regis Philbin
D) Bob Barker

11. Which film won the Academy Award for Best Picture in 1984
A) The Terminator
B) Beverly Hills Cop
C) Ghostbusters
D) Terms of Endearment

12. Who won the Academy Award for Best Actress in a Leading Role for her performance in "Terms of Endearment"?
A) Meryl Streep
B) Shirley MacLaine
C) Diane Keaton
D) Glenn Close

Chapter 3:
Music: Top Songs, Albums, and Awards

In the vibrant world of music, the year 1984 witnessed chart-toppers, musical trends, and remarkable honors that left an indelible mark on the industry. Let's dive into the melodious journey of '84:

3.1 Chart-Toppers and Musical Trends

1. Chart-Toppers

1984 was a year when the airwaves were filled with catchy tunes and emerging musical trends. Some of the chart-topping hits that had everyone singing along included:

"When Doves Cry" by Prince:

Prince's enigmatic and genre-defying hit became an anthem of the '80s, blending rock, pop, and funk in a unique way.

"Like a Virgin" by Madonna:
Madonna's provocative yet irresistible single solidified her status as the Queen of Pop, sparking discussions and dance parties alike.

"Careless Whisper" by George Michael:
George Michael's soulful ballad captured hearts worldwide, showcasing his remarkable vocal talent.

"I Want to Know What Love Is" by Foreigner:

This power ballad struck a chord with listeners, resonating with its emotive lyrics and powerful melodies.

"Jump" by Van Halen:

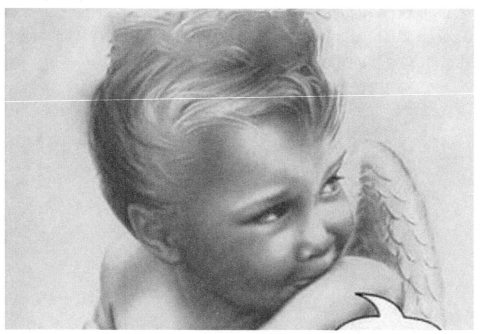

Van Halen's electrifying rock anthem had audiences jumping to its infectious guitar riffs and energetic rhythm.

"Wake Me Up Before You Go-Go" by Wham!:

Wham!'s upbeat and colorful track became a pop sensation, inspiring legions of fans to dance along.

2. Musical Trends

The musical landscape of 1984 was a vibrant tapestry of diverse genres and emerging trends that left an indelible mark on the decade. Here's a deeper look at the musical **trends that defined the year:**

Synthpop Dominance:

One of the most significant musical trends of 1984 was the continued dominance of synthpop. Synthesizers, electronic drums, and innovative production techniques created a futuristic and often dreamy sound that characterized many chart-topping hits. Artists like Madonna, Prince, and Eurythmics embraced this genre, delivering iconic tracks that fused pop sensibilities with electronic elements. Songs like Madonna's "Like a Virgin" and Prince's "When Doves Cry" exemplified the synthpop sound that was ruling the airwaves.

New Wave Evolution:

Duran Duran

While new wave had been on the scene since the late '70s, it continued to evolve in 1984. Bands like Duran Duran, The Cars, and Culture Club expanded their sound, incorporating elements of funk, dance, and rock into their music. New wave's catchy melodies, quirky lyrics, and stylish visuals made it a defining genre of the '80s.

Glam Metal Emergence:

1984 marked the emergence of glam metal or "hair metal." Bands like Van Halen and Motley Crue brought a flamboyant and rebellious energy to rock music. Characterized by flashy stage attire, big hair, and anthemic guitar solos, glam metal would go on to dominate the late '80s music scene.

3.2 Music Awards and Honors

In the world of music awards and honors, 1984 witnessed outstanding achievements and recognition. Some of the notable accolades included:

The 26th Annual Grammy Awards celebrated musical excellence, with Michael Jackson's "Beat It" winning Record of the Year.

Michael Jackson

MTV Video Music Awards recognized groundbreaking music videos, with "Thriller" by Michael Jackson becoming an iconic presence.

The American Music Awards honored artists across various genres, with Lionel Richie taking home multiple awards, including Favorite Pop/Rock Male Artist.

Lionel Richie

The Rock and Roll Hall of Fame inducted legendary artists like The Beatles and Bob Dylan, cementing their status as musical pioneers.

Activity: Music Lyrics Challenge – Guess the Song Lyrics from '84

Test your knowledge of '84 music with this fun lyrics challenge! See if you can match the lyrics to the songs mentioned in the chapter.

1. "You don't have to be rich to be my girl, you don't have to be cool to rule my world."

Song: _____

2. "I made it through the wilderness, somehow I made it through."

Song: _____

3. "I'm never gonna dance again, guilty feet have got no rhythm."

Song: _____

4. "You are the sunshine of my life, that's why I'll always be around."

Song: _____

5. "Might as well jump! Go ahead and jump."

Song: _____

6. "Last Christmas, I gave you my heart, but the very next day, you gave it away."

Song: _____

7. "In a world that must be strong, 'cause true love, it conquers all."

Song: _____

8. "She's a very kinky girl, the kind you don't take home to mother."

Song: _____

8. "She's a very kinky girl, the kind you don't take home to mother."

Song: _____

9. "Girls just wanna have fun, oh girls just wanna have fun."

Song: _____

10. "Sweet child o' mine, oh, yeah, yeah."

Song: _____

Chapter 4: Sports in 1984
A Journey Through the World of Athletics

Sports have always held a special place in the hearts of people around the world, and the year 1984 was no exception. From the grandeur of the Olympic Games to the nail-biting moments in American sports, this chapter takes you on a thrilling journey through the athletic achievements and memorable victories of '84.

4.1 Athletic Achievements and Memorable Victories

1. Olympic Games:

The Summer Olympic Games are held in Los Angeles

The 1984 Summer Olympics, also known as the Games of the XXIII Olympiad, begin in July. The games were held in Los Angeles, California. There were a total of 6,829 athletes who participated in 221 events and represented 140 different countries. As retaliation for the United States' boycott of the 1980 Moscow Olympics, The Soviet Union and several other countries boycotted these games. Despite the boycott, there was still record participation. Some events that were included for the first time in these games were the women's marathon, women's cycling road race, synchronized swimming, rhythmic gymnastics, and windsurfing. The United States won the most medals with a total of 174, followed by Romania and West Germany.

The Winter Olympic Games are held in Sarajevo, Yugoslavia

The 1984 Winter Olympics were held in Sarajevo, Yugoslavia from February 8th to February 19th, 1984. It was the first time that the Winter Olympics were held in a socialist and Slavic-speaking country. The event saw the participation of nearly 1,300 athletes from 49 countries who competed in 39 events across 10 sports. The opening ceremony was held at the Koševo Stadium and was attended by 50,000 spectators and watched by over 2 billion television viewers worldwide. East Germany topped the gold medal count with nine medals, three more than the Soviet Union, which had led this count in the past three Games. The Soviet delegation won the most overall medals (25), including the most silvers (10) and bronzes (9)

2. UEFA European Championship:

The 1984 UEFA European Football Championship final tournament was held in France from June 12th to June 27th, 1984.
It was the seventh UEFA European Championship, a competition held every four years and endorsed by UEFA. At the
time, only eight countries took part in the final stage of the
tournament, seven of which had to come through the quali-
fying stage. France qualified automatically as hosts of the
event; in the tournament led by Michel Platini, who scored
nine goals in France's five matches, Les Bleus won the champi
onship – their first major international title

3. US Masters Golf:

April 15 witnessed a legendary moment in golf history as Ben Crenshaw secured the coveted green jacket at the 48th US Masters Tournament, held at Augusta National Golf Club. His two-stroke victory over the likes of Tom Watson, a champion in 1977 and 1981, showcased the resilience and precision required to conquer one of the sport's most prestigious events.

Ben Crenshaw

4. Wimbledon Tennis:

On the hallowed grass courts of Wimbledon, the spirit of tennis reigned supreme. John McEnroe's triumphant third Wimbledon title echoed with the thunderous applause of spectators, while Martina Navratilova's historic sixth Wimbledon victory and fourth consecutive US Open title showcased her unparalleled prowess on the tennis court. Their victories became chapters in the storied history of tennis, etching their names in gold.

5. F1 World Champion:

Oct 21 Austrian Ferrari driver Niki Lauda becomes a 3-time Formula 1 World Drivers champion when he finishes 2nd in the season ending Portuguese Grand Prix at Estoril; wins title by just 0.5 from Alain Prost

4.2 American Sports: Champions and Championship Moments

The Super Bowl, the pinnacle of American football, witnessed an iconic showdown in 1984. The Los Angeles Raiders emerged as champions, conquering the Washington Redskins with a resounding score of 38-9. It was a moment of gridiron glory, with heroes and champions etching their names in the annals of American sports.

2. NBA Finals:

In the world of basketball, the 1984 NBA Finals was an intense battle of skill, strategy, and sheer determination. The Boston Celtics clinched the championship by defeating the Los Angeles Lakers in a thrilling seven-game series. Each dribble, pass, and dunk added to the drama, making it a championship series for the ages.

3. World Series:

On the baseball diamond, the Detroit Tigers soared to victory in the 1984 World Series, besting the San Diego Padres in a five-game series. Their triumph was a testament to the power of teamwork, precision, and the pursuit of excellence that defines America's pastime.

4. Stanley Cup:

Ice hockey enthusiasts rejoiced as the Edmonton Oilers secured the Stanley Cup in 1984, defeating the New York Islanders. It was a moment of icy brilliance, with the Oilers capturing their first-ever Stanley Cup and etching their names in the history of the sport.

Activity: Sports Trivia –
Test Your Knowledge of 1984 Sports History

1. Which city hosted the 1984 Summer Olympics?

A.   Los Angeles

B.   Moscow

C.   Seoul

D.   Tokyo

2. Why did several countries, including the Soviet Union, boycott the 1984 Summer Olympics?

A.   Political conflicts

B.   Economic reasons

C.   Concerns about athlete safety

D.   In protest of the host country

3. Where were the 1984 Winter Olympics held?

Lake Placid, USA

A.   Calgary, Canada

B.   Sarajevo, Yugoslavia

C.   Innsbruck, Austria

4. Which country finished first on the medal table at the 1984 Winter Olympics?

A.   United States

B.   Soviet Union

C.   East Germany

D.   Canada

5. Who won the 1984 UEFA European Football Championship?

A.   France

B.   Germany

C.   Italy

D.   Spain

6. Who won the 1984 US Masters Tournament at Augusta National Golf Club?

A. Tom Watson

B. Ben Crenshaw

C. Arnold Palmer

D. Jack Nicklaus

7. How many Wimbledon titles did John McEnroe win in 1984?

A. One

B. Two

C. Three

D. None

8. Who secured their fourth consecutive US Open title in 1984?

A. John McEnroe

B. Bjorn Borg

C. Martina Navratilova

D. Chris Evert

9. Who became the Formula 1 World Drivers' Champion in 1984?

A. Niki Lauda

B. Alain Prost

C. Ayrton Senna

D. Michael Schumacher

10. Which team won Super Bowl XVIII in 1984?

A. Los Angeles Raiders

B. Washington Redskins

C. San Francisco 49ers

D. Miami Dolphins

11. Who won the NBA Finals in 1984?

A.   Boston Celtics

B.   Los Angeles Lakers

C.   Chicago Bulls

D.   Detroit Pistons

12. Which baseball team triumphed in the 1984 World Series?

A.   New York Yankees

B.   Los Angeles Dodgers

C.   Detroit Tigers

D.   San Diego Padres

13. Who won the Stanley Cup in 1984?

A.   Edmonton Oilers

B.   New York Islanders

C.   Montreal Canadiens

D.   Chicago Blackhawks

Chapter 5:
Pop Culture, Fashion,
and Popular Leisure Activities

In the vibrant tapestry of 1984's pop culture, fashion made bold statements, and leisure activities brought joy to people's lives. Let's step into the world of '84:

5.1 Fashion Flashback: What the World Wore in '84

The fashion landscape of 1984 was a blend of diverse styles that reflected the spirit of the era. Here's a glimpse of what the world wore:

1. Members Only Jackets

These sleek, often sleekly styled jackets were a symbol of cool sophistication. With their signature epaulets and ribbed collars, Members Only jackets were a must-have for anyone looking to exude an air of effortless style.

2. Original Jams:

Original Jams were a colorful and playful take on shorts. Featuring bold, eye-catching patterns and vibrant hues, they perfectly captured the carefree spirit of the '80s.

3. Parachute Pants:

Parachute pants, often made of synthetic materials, were known for their baggy, puffy appearance. They were a dance floor favorite, allowing for freedom of movement and a futuristic look.

4. Converse Chucks:

Chuck Taylor All-Stars by Converse were the quintessential sneakers of '84. These classic, canvas shoes were loved by both athletes and fashion-conscious individuals, becoming an enduring footwear choice.

5. Reebok Hightops:

Reebok's high-top sneakers were another fashion staple. With their distinctive Velcro straps and athletic aesthetic, they were synonymous with the burgeoning fitness culture of the '80s.

6. Denim Everywhere:

Denim was a wardrobe essential in 1984. From acid-washed jeans to denim jackets, this versatile fabric was a fashion staple for people of all ages.

8. Swatch Watches:

Swatch watches combined functionality with bold, artistic designs. These affordable and stylish timepieces allowed wearers to express their personality through their wrists.

9. Wayfarer Sunglasses:

Ray-Ban Wayfarer sunglasses had a resurgence in popularity in '84. Their distinctive shape and bold frames became a fashion statement, favored by trendsetters and celebrities alike.

10. Big Teased-Up Hair:

'84 was all about big hair. Both men and women experimented with voluminous hairstyles, using hairspray and teasing combs to achieve gravity-defying looks. The bigger, the better!

5.2 Entertainment and Hobbies

In the realm of entertainment and leisure, '84 offered a plethora of activities and pastimes that captured the hearts and minds of people around the world:

1. Video Games:

Duck hunt

The video game industry was booming in 1984, with iconic games like "Tetris" and "Duck Hunt" captivating gamers. Home consoles, including the Nintendo Entertainment System (NES) brought arcade-quality gaming to living rooms.

2. Personal Computers:

Personal computers, like the Apple Macintosh, were becoming more accessible to the general public. The introduction of graphical user interfaces (GUIs) made these computers more user-friendly and expanded their applications beyond business and education.

3. Roller Skating:

Roller skating rinks were popular hangout spots, where people of all ages glided to the rhythm of disco and pop music. Roller disco, characterized by flashy outfits and groovy moves, was a particularly beloved trend.

4. VHS Tapes:

The widespread availability of VHS tapes revolutionized home entertainment. Families could rent or purchase movies, bringing the cinematic experience to their living rooms.

5. Aerobics:

The fitness craze of the '80s introduced aerobics as a fun and effective way to stay in shape. Exercise videos led by enthusiastic instructors became a common sight in homes across the world.

6. Music Mixtapes:

Creating mixtapes by recording songs from the radio or viny records onto cassette tapes was a popular way to curate per sonalized music collections.

7. Trivial Pursuit:

Board games like Trivial Pursuit became favorite pastimes for gatherings with friends and family. Testing knowledge and quick thinking, these games provided hours of entertainment.

Activity:
Fashion Design Coloring Page
Create Your '84-Inspired Outfit

Share your 1984 photos,
Don't forget to show off your fabulous '80s fashion!

Chapter 6:
Technological Advancements and Popular Cars

6.1 Innovations That Shaped the Future

The year 1984 witnessed a wave of groundbreaking innovations that would go on to shape the future in various fields, from technology to healthcare and beyond. Here are some of the remarkable innovations that left an indelible mark on history:

Aids Virus identified by French Immunologist

.In 1984, a monumental discovery in the field of medicine occurred when French immunologist Luc Montagnier identified the human immunodeficiency virus (HIV), which is responsible for acquired immunodeficiency syndrome (AIDS).

.This crucial breakthrough paved the way for further research into the virus, its transmission, and ultimately, the development of treatments and preventive measures for AIDS.

AT&T Broken Up

.The year 1984 marked a significant turning point in the telecommunications industry as the U.S. Department of Justice ordered the breakup of the American Telephone and Telegraph Company (AT&T).

.This landmark decision led to the divestiture of AT&T into several regional companies, opening the door to increased competition and innovation in the telecommunications sector.

The first Apple Macintosh goes on sale

.January 24, 1984, marked the introduction of the Apple Macintosh, a personal computer that would revolutionize the way people interacted with technology.

.With its iconic Super Bowl commercial and graphical user interface, the Macintosh set new standards for user-friendly computing, laying the foundation for the modern computing experience.

Sony and Philips introduce the first commercial CD Players

.In a collaborative effort, Sony and Philips introduced the first commercial compact disc (CD) players in 1984.
.These devices brought digital audio into homes, offering high-quality sound and improved durability compared to traditional vinyl records and cassette tapes.

Sony makes the first 3 1/2" computer disk

.Sony's innovation extended to data storage with the introduction of the 3 1/2" computer diskette, also known as the "floppy disk."
.This compact and durable storage medium became a standard for personal computers and played a crucial role in data transfer and backup for years to come.

Genetic Fingerprinting (DNA Profiling) Developed:

.One of the most significant innovations in forensic science occurred in 1984 with the development of genetic fingerprin ing, also known as DNA profiling.

.This groundbreaking technique allowed forensic scientists to analyze an individual's unique DNA characteristics, revo- lutionizing criminal investigations and providing a more accu- rate means of identifying suspects and solving crimes.

Space Shuttle Discovery maiden flight:

The Space Shuttle Discovery launches for its maiden flight on August 30th, 1984. It was the third of the space shuttles to be put into operation after the Columbia and the Challenger. The Discovery launched for the first time from the Kennedy Space Center in Florida and was in space until September 5th, 1984 when it landed at the Edwards Air Force Base in California. The crew consisted of five men and one woman. The mission was originally planned to launch in June but various technical issues pushed the launch date back.

6.2 The Automobiles of '84

As the automotive industry continued to innovate, 1984 saw the release of iconic cars that captured the spirit of the era. From sleek sports cars to family-friendly models, this section explores the automobiles that graced the roads in '84.

Chevrolet Corvette C4:

The Chevrolet Corvette C4, introduced in 1984, was a beacon of American automotive excellence. With its aerodynamic design, digital instrumentation, and potent V8 engine, the Corvette C4 appealed to sports car enthusiasts and set a new standard for performance and style.

Ford Mustang SVO:

Ford's Mustang SVO (Special Vehicle Operations) combined the classic appeal of the Mustang with modern performance. It featured a turbocharged four-cylinder engine, sport-tuned suspension, and distinctive styling cues. The Mustang SVO catered to drivers seeking both power and precision.

Toyota Camry:

The 1984 Toyota Camry represented a shift towards practicality and reliability. This midsize sedan emphasized fuel efficiency, comfort, and dependability, making it a popular choice among families and commuters. The Camry's reputation for quality would endure for decades to come.

Honda CRX:

Honda's CRX was a compact and sporty hatchback that offered an engaging driving experience. Its lightweight design, responsive handling, and fuel-efficient engine made it a hit with drivers looking for a fun and economical ride.

Chrysler minivans:

Dodge Caravan 1984

Plymouth Voyager Minivan 1984

Chrysler introduced the Dodge Caravan and Plymouth Voyager minivans in 1984, revolutionizing family transportation. These innovative vehicles offered spacious interiors, versatile seating arrangements, and sliding doors, setting the stage for the minivan's enduring popularity.

Activity:
Car logo quiz - Guess the car logo

1._____

2._____

3._____

4._____

5._____

6._____

Chapter 7:
Stats and the Cost of Things

In 1984, the cost of living and consumer prices reflected the economic landscape of the time. Here's a glimpse into the price tags for various items and expenses in '84:

7.1 The Price Tag: Cost of Living in 1984

. Average Cost of new house $86,730

. Median Price Of and Existing Home $72,400
. Average Income per year $21,600.00
. Average Monthly Rent $350.00
. Movie Ticket $2.50

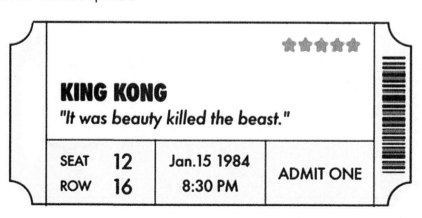

. 1 gallon of gas $1.10

. Dodge RAM 50 Truck $8,995.00

. Chrysler New Yorker $13,045

. Mens   Leather   Shoes $39.99

. Chicago, Illinois
Brick Tudor 3 bedroom all modern appliances double garage sundeck $119,000

. Chevrolet Corvette $23,392
. Apples Lb 43 cents

. Bacon Lb $1.69

7.2 Dollars and Sense: Inflation and Its Effects

In 1984, the economic climate was shaped by several key indicators that provided insights into the financial landscape of the year:

1. Yearly Inflation Rate (USA): 4.3%

Inflation, the rate at which the general level of prices for goods and services rises, was a significant economic factor in 1984. The United States experienced an annual inflation rate of 4.3% during this period. This meant that, on average, the prices of everyday goods and services increased by 4.3% over the course of the year.

The effects of inflation were felt by consumers as their purchasing power diminished. As prices rose, the cost of living increased, impacting households' budgets and spending habits. It also influenced financial planning and investment decisions as individuals and businesses sought ways to protect their assets from eroding due to rising prices.

2. Year-End Close Dow Jones: 1211

The Dow Jones Industrial Average (DJIA), a key stock market index that measures the performance of 30 large, publicly-owned companies, closed the year at a value of 1211. The year-end close of the Dow Jones was an important indicator of the stock market's performance and investor sentiment.

A year-end close of 1211 suggested that the stock market had experienced growth and positive returns over the course of the year. Investors may have seen opportunities for investment in various sectors, and businesses may have used this indicator to gauge economic conditions and plan for the future.

3. Interest Rates (Year-End Federal Reserve): 10.75%

The Federal Reserve, the central banking system of the United States, plays a crucial role in managing the country's monetary policy. In 1984, the Federal Reserve set the year-end interest rate at 10.75%. This interest rate, often referred to as the federal funds rate, influenced borrowing costs, lending rates, and overall economic activity.

A year-end interest rate of 10.75% indicated that the Federal Reserve was using monetary policy tools to manage inflation and stabilize the economy. Higher interest rates can encourage saving and discourage borrowing, which can help control inflation but may also slow down economic growth.

Activity:
1984 Shopping List Challenge

Instructions:

. Below, you'll find a list of common household items and groceries that were available in 1984. We've included the approximate prices these items would have cost during that time.

. Your task is to create your own shopping list by selecting items from the provided list. Imagine you're shopping in 1984, and choose the items you would need for your daily life.

. Next to each selected item, write down the 1984 price. You can use the provided prices as a reference or conduct your own research to estimate the costs.

. Calculate the total cost of your shopping list based on the 1984 prices. Take a moment to compare this cost with today's prices for the same items, if you wish.

. Share your reflections on the activity. What surprised you the most about the cost differences between 1984 and today? How do you think these changes have affected people's lives?

☐ Apples, Granny Smith, .69/lb
☐ Bacon, Shop Rite, 1.69/lb
☐ Beans, baked, Hanover .99/4 14.5 oz cans
☐ Beef, ground, extra lean, 1.87/lb
☐ Bread, .59/20 oz loaf
☐ Cereal, Kellogg's Rice Krispies, 1.89/19 oz box
☐ Cheese, Borden singles, 1.89/lb

- ☐ Chicken, Purdue Oven Stuffer, .79/lb
- ☐ Coffee, Hills Brothers, 1.79/13 oz can
- ☐ Cookies, Nabisco Oreos, 1.89/20 oz pkg
- ☐ Corn, Green Giant, .63/12 oz can
- ☐ Eggs, .89/dozen
- ☐ Fish, cod fillets, fresh, 1.99/lb
- ☐ Hot dogs, Oscar Mayer, 1.39/lb
- ☐ Ice cream, Dolly Madison, 1.99/half gallon
- ☐ Juice, Hawaiian Punch, .59/46 oz can
- ☐ Juice, orange, Minute Maid, 1.69/half gallon
- ☐ Ketchup, Heinz, 1.19/32 oz bottle
- ☐ Margarine, Land O Lakes, .39/lb
- ☐ Mayonnaise, Kraft, 1.59/quart jar
- ☐ Lettuce, large head, .49/each
- ☐ Oranges, Jaffa, .99/5
- ☐ Peanut butter, Peter Pan, 1.29/18 oz jar
- ☐ Potatoes, Idaho, 1.29/5 lb bag
- ☐ Preserves, Welch's grape, .99/2 lb jar
- ☐ Soda, Sprite, .99/2 litre bottle
- ☐ Spaghetti, Prince, 1.00/3 one pound boxes
- ☐ Tea, Salada, 1.79/100 count box
- ☐ Tuna, Starkist, solid pack, oil or water, .89/6.5 oz can

☐			
☐			
☐			
☐			
☐			
☐			
☐			
☐			
☐			
☐			
☐			
☐			
☐			
☐			
☐			
☐			
☐			
☐			
☐			
		Total	

Chapter 8:
The Famous Wedding and Divorce of 1984

8.1 Famous weddings

Love was in the air in 1984 as several famous couples celebrated their unions, capturing the hearts of the public and the media. Here are some of the notable weddings that took place during the year:

Andrew Lloyd Webber & Sarah Brightman

On March 22, composer Andrew Lloyd Webber, at the age of 36, exchanged vows with the talented singer and dancer Sarah Brightman, who was 23 at the time. The picturesque setting for their wedding was Hampshire, England. This union brought together two prominent figures in the world of music and theater, and their love story would continue to evolve in the spotlight.

Diego Maradona & Claudia Villafañe

FIFA soccer legend Diego Maradona, aged 24, tied the knot with his long-time fiancée Claudia Villafañe in a glamorous wedding ceremony held in Buenos Aires on November 7. The union of Maradona, renowned for his extraordinary skills on the soccer field, and Claudia marked a significant moment in both their lives, celebrated by fans and well-wishers.

Roger Clemens & Debra Lynn Godfrey

Major League Baseball pitcher Roger Clemens, just 22 years old at the time, stepped up to the plate in his personal life on November 24 as he exchanged wedding vows with Debra Lynn Godfrey. The ceremony was a private affair, and it marked a new chapter in Clemens' life beyond the baseball diamond.

Sally Field & Alan Greisman

Academy Award-winning actress Sally Field chose December 15 to embark on a new journey as she wed her second husband, Alan Greisman. The wedding marked a personal milestone for Field, known for her exceptional acting talent and captivating performances on screen.

Paul O'Neill & Nevalee Davis

On December 29, Major League Baseball player Paul O'Neill, aged 21, married his childhood sweetheart Nevalee Davis. Their love story began in Columbus, Ohio, and their wedding in the same city was a heartwarming celebration of their enduring connection.

8.2 Famous divorces

While love found its way into the hearts of many in 1984, for some, it was a year marked by the end of significant relationships. Here are some of the notable divorces that took place during the year:

Pierre Trudeau & Margaret Sinclair

On April 2, Canadian Prime Minister Pierre Trudeau, aged 64, and his wife Margaret Sinclair, 35, officially ended their marriage due to irreconcilable differences. Their divorce came after 13 years of marriage and attracted widespread attention, given Trudeau's status as a prominent political figure in Canada. The dissolution of their union marked a significant personal chapter for both individuals.

John Carpenter & Adrienne Barbeau

Film director John Carpenter, 36, and actress Adrienne Barbeau, 39, decided to part ways on September 14, ending their marriage of five years. Both Carpenter and Barbeau were well-known figures in the entertainment industry, making their divorce a matter of interest among fans and followers.

George Gervin & Joyce King

NBA guard George Gervin, aged 32, and Joyce King, his spouse of nearly eight years, parted ways on October 16. Their divorce marked the conclusion of a significant period in their lives, and it was observed by fans of the basketball star.

Kate Jackson & David Greenwald

Actress Kate Jackson, 36, and business executive David Greenwald separated, finalizing their divorce on December 20. Their union, which lasted two years, came to an end, signifying a personal transition for both individuals

Activity:
Wedding and Divorce Timeline Challenge

In this activity, you will test your knowledge of famous weddings and divorces that occurred in the year 1984. Match the couples to their respective events by placing the correct wedding or divorce date next to their names. Let's see how well you remember these celebrity unions and separations from '84!

Weddings:
1. Diego Maradona & Claudia Villafañe: [Wedding Date]
2. Paul O'Neill & Nevalee Davis: [Wedding Date]
3. Roger Clemens & Debra Lynn Godfrey: [Wedding Date]
4. Andrew Lloyd Webber & Sarah Brightman: [Wedding Date]
5. Sally Field & Alan Greisman: [Wedding Date]

Divorces:
1. Kate Jackson & David Greenwald: [Divorce Date]
2. John Carpenter & Adrienne Barbeau: [Divorce Date]
3. George Gervin & Joyce King: [Divorce Date]

Unleash your creativity and bring the famous 1984 wedding to life with vibrant colors in this exciting coloring wedding picture activity

Relaxing Corner
1984 Review Crossword

Instructions:

Solve the crossword by filling in the blanks with the correct words or phrases related to the events and facts of 1974. Read the book or use your knowledge of the year 1974 to complete the crossword.

Have fun and test your memory!

Crossword Clues:

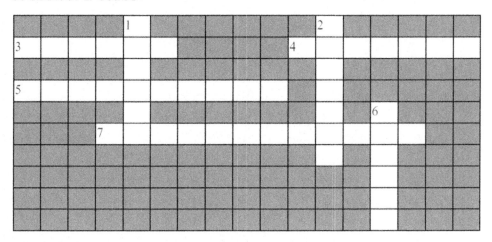

ACROSS

3. The famous TV show set in a bar where "everybody knows your name."

4. The singer who released the provocative hit "Like a Virgin."

5. The city where the 1984 Summer Olympics were held.

7. The legendary filmmaker who directed "Star Trek III: The Search for Spock."

DOWN

1. The iconic musician known for the hit "When Doves Cry."
2. The British and Irish musicians who formed "Band Aid" to raise money for famine relief in Ethiopia.
6. The sport in which Diego Maradona was a legendary figure.

Special gift for readers

We have heartfelt thank-you gifts for you
As a token of our appreciation for joining us on this historical journey through 1984, we've included a set of cards and stamps inspired by the year of 1984. These cards are your canvas to capture the essence of the past. We encourage you to use them as inspiration for creating your own unique cards, sharing your perspective on the historical moments we've explored in this book. Whether it's a holiday greeting or a simple hello to a loved one, these cards are your way to connect with the history we've uncovered together.

Happy creating!

Activity Answers:

Chapter 1:

ACROSS:
4. BURGER
5. ENGLAND
6. SCARGILL
7. ETHIOPIA
8. INDIRA
9. ZHAOZIYANG
DOWN:
1. THATCHER
2. BRANSON
3. SELASSIE
4. BHOPAL

Chapter 2:

1. B) Ivan Reitman
2. A) Harrison Ford
3. C) Mogwai
4. A) Eddie Murphy
5. A) Karate
6. C) Magnum, P.I.
7. A) The Carringtons
8. C) Entertainment Tonight
9. C) Police procedural
10. B) Alex Trebek
11. D) Terms of Endearment
12. B) Shirley MacLaine

Chapter 3:

1. Song: "Kiss" by Prince
2. Song: "Like a Virgin" by Madonna
3. Song: "Careless Whisper" by George Michael
4. Song: "You Are the Sunshine of My Life" by Stevie Wonder
5. Song: "Jump" by Van Halen
6. Song: "Last Christmas" by Wham!
7. Song: "I Want to Know What Love Is" by Foreigner
8. Song: "Super Freak" by Rick James
9. Song: "Girls Just Want to Have Fun" by Cyndi Lauper
10. Song: "Sweet Child o' Mine" by Guns N' Roses

Chapter 4:

1. Los Angeles
2. In protest of the host country
3. Sarajevo, Yugoslavia
4. East Germany
5. France
6. Ben Crenshaw
7. Three
8. Martina Navratilova
9. Niki Lauda
10. Los Angeles Raiders
11. Boston Celtics
12. Detroit Tigers
13. Edmonton Oilers

Chapter 6:

1. Chrysler
2. Chevrolet
3. Honda
4. Toyota
5. Ford
6. Mercedes-Benz

Chapter 7:

Weddings:
1. Diego Maradona & Claudia Villafañe: November 7
2. Paul O'Neill & Nevalee Davis: December 29
3. Roger Clemens & Debra Lynn Godfrey: November 24
4. Andrew Lloyd Webber & Sarah Brightman: March 22
5. Sally Field & Alan Greisman: December 15
Divorces:
1. Kate Jackson & David Greenwald: December 20
2. John Carpenter & Adrienne Barbeau: September 14
3. George Gervin & Joyce King: October 16
4. Pierre Trudeau & Margaret Sinclair: April 2

Relaxing corner:

1. Prince
2. BandAid
3. Cheers
4. Madonna
5. LosAngeles
6. Soccer
7. LeonardNimoy

Embracing 1984: A Grateful Farewell

Thank you for joining us on this journey through a year that holds a special place in our hearts. Whether you experienced 1984 firsthand or through the pages of this book, we hope it brought you moments of joy, nostalgia, and connection to a time that will forever shine brightly in our memories.

Share Your Thoughts and Help Us Preserve History

Your support and enthusiasm for this journey mean the world to us. We invite you to share your thoughts, leave a review, and keep the spirit of '84 alive. As we conclude our adventure, we look forward to more journeys through the annals of history together. Until then, farewell and thank you for the memories.

We would like to invite you to explore more of our fantastic world by scanning the QR code below. There you can easily get free ebooks from us and receive so many surprises.

TO DO LIST

- ○ --------------------------------------
- ○ --------------------------------------
- ○ --------------------------------------
- ○ --------------------------------------
- ○ --------------------------------------
- ○ --------------------------------------
- ○ --------------------------------------
- ○ --------------------------------------
- ○ --------------------------------------
- ○ --------------------------------------
- ○ --------------------------------------
- ○ --------------------------------------
- ○ --------------------------------------
- ○ --------------------------------------

well done!

To Do List

- [ ]
- [ ]
- [ ]
- [ ]
- [ ]
- [ ]
- [ ]
- [ ]
- [ ]
- [ ]
- [ ]
- [ ]
- [ ]
- [ ]
- [ ]

To Do List

- [ ] _____
- [ ] _____
- [ ] _____
- [ ] _____
- [ ] _____
- [ ] _____
- [ ] _____
- [ ] _____
- [ ] _____
- [ ] _____
- [ ] _____
- [ ] _____
- [ ] _____
- [ ] _____

TO DO LIST

- ○ --
- ○ --
- ○ --
- ○ --
- ○ --
- ○ --
- ○ --
- ○ --
- ○ --
- ○ --
- ○ --
- ○ --
- ○ --
- ○ --

well
done!

TO DO LIST

Name: _____ Day: _____ Month: _____

No	To Do List	Yes	No

TO DO LIST

Name: _____   Day: _____   Month: _____

No	To Do List	Yes	No

TO DO LIST

Name: _____ Day: _____ Month: _____

No	To Do List	Yes	No

TO DO LIST

Name: _____   Day: _____   Month: _____

No	To Do List	Yes	No

NOTE

NOTE

NOTE

NOTE

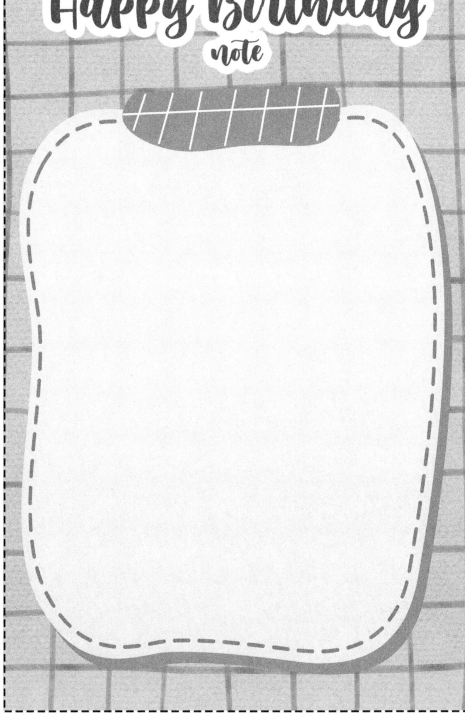

Happy Birthday
note

Happy Birthday
note

HAPPY BIRTHDAY NOTE

POSTCARD

Correspondence

Address

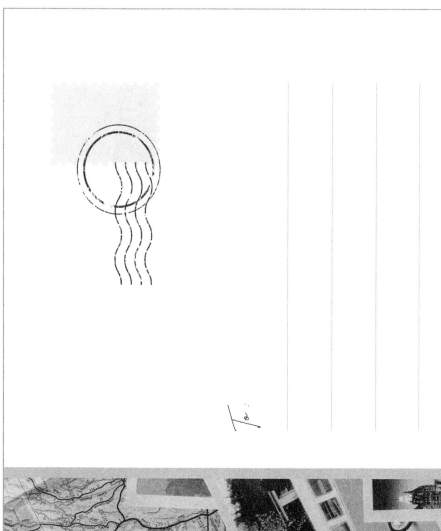

Remember This!

WISH YOU WERE HERE,
123 ANYWHERE ST., ANY CITY

POSTCARD

To:

From:

Printed in Great Britain
by Amazon